Priceless Tips at Your Fingertips: **Email Overload**

By

Sudhir Diddee

Copyright and Disclaimer

Send comments to diddee@outlook.com

ISBN-13: 978- 1499396423

ISBN-10: 1499396422

Library of Congress Control Number: 2014908611

To all office workers overwhelmed by e-mail

Acknowledgements

I have been fortunate to work in a great company, and was inspired by Microsoft co-founder Bill Gates' book, Business @ the Speed of Thought: Succeeding in the Digital Economy? What I have learned in Microsoft is the rigorous product development process and the years of user research on work and productivity that went into each feature design. The final products are awesome; however, given the plethora of features, users don't usually get around to using all of them. If you added the incremental productivity gained from all the features, you would be significantly better off. The same is true of its email product, Outlook®; you can save significant time each day by investing a small amount of time now in learning the features contained in Outlook®.

I would like to thank my editor Leigh-Anne, and my designer Kris Hamper. I also credit the wonderful executives, smart managers and terrific colleagues, too many to list here, with whom I am fortunate to work with and learn from every day, and who make my company truly the best place to work.

Finally, I would like to thank my wife and my kids for being extremely patient as I worked to write this book in bits and pieces. As any author knows, writing a book is hard work, and finishing the book is even harder, given all of the other priorities in life. Like everything in life, it is the result of trade-offs we make to prioritize the things we want to achieve. This book is largely about priorities, and saving time on e-mail so that you can return to the more interesting things that life holds for you. I hope this book will add value (and time!) to your life.

Table of Contents

Intended Audience

This book is intended for the average office worker who is overwhelmed by email. If you are anyone who spends more than hour a day on email you will benefit the most, not only from the tips, but also by the system proposed in this book.

More than anything, this is a system of managing email, along with the right set up and most importantly the discipline needed to follow through on your resolution. The software I have used to illustrate the examples in this book is Outlook® 2013, but most of the tips should work on Outlook® 2010 or earlier versions as well. Some of the tips have been working for years; users just aren't aware or don't use them.

In my experience, most modern-day office workers are familiar with some features of commonly used software. However, either due to lack of time or being afraid to try new things, we stop pushing ourselves. Modern software allow us to **DO MORE,** provided you want to and are willing to commit to Do More. With software, the sky is the limit and literally no one can call themselves an expert, as the boundaries are being pushed all the time at a pace that is impossible to keep up with.

One of the challenges in learning is to **implement the learning** at work. I am an avid reader and I find that translating the skills learned in books to my actual work life takes a lot of conscious effort and is extremely hard. I would love for my users to learn from me, and to follow these steps and implement what they learn much more easily.

How to use this book

This book is intended more to show a **system of managing email overload** than a book that teaches you e-mail tools and hidden features. It aims to shed light on all aspects of e-mail, including the bad habits of checking e-mail several times a day.

The skills are in an increasing order of difficulty, and while some tips should be familiar to many users, even the advanced user should still find about 15 to 20 new tips.

As with everything in life, changing old habits is hard. The same is true for benefiting from the tips in this book. Various research scholars on human behavior have suggested that it takes 21 days to form a habit. I think that is a good benchmark. The best way to use this book is to take any one section at a time and practice the tips till they become second nature.

You should review the section on **The Outlook® Graphical User Interface** in the Appendix to familiarize yourself with the elements of a program window, to make the most of these tips. Take a printout of the Cheat Sheet at the end of the book and pin it next to your computer at work and at home. Every so often while doing email, check yourself to see if you have fallen back to doing it the old way. Soon you will be addicted to the new method(s)!

Finally, the best way to learn is to teach others, and to push yourself to take on harder problems. There is no substitute for practice. Remember to be curious. There is a community of passionate users out there willing to teach and to learn. This work itself stands on the shoulders of giants, since I have learned these over the years through friends, colleagues, websites and sheer curiosity. If you come across a valuable tip, please feel free to e-mail me at: diddee@outlook.com

The E-mail menace

This book is about a system of e-mail management. It covers five sections: E-mail Basics, E-mail Setup, E-mail Management, E-mail Delegation, E-mail Best Practices and Advanced Techniques. It will require some initial effort from you to set up your e-mail in this new format. From then on, it will require disciple and repeated practice of the e-mail management and best practices, for you to make the most of this book. **Read this book only if you are committed to ending e-mail slavery! This will give you back the most precious gift of all: time.** For most folks it is not about the e-mail, it is what to do with the extra time! An alternate view might be to look at 5 things you want to accomplish, and very deliberately carve out time for it; e.g.: I want to find time to exercise 20 minutes a day, I want to learn all about a new part of the business, I want more time for networking with people. This will provide you with inspiration for your hard work to tame your email.

Needless to say, we live in a world that is exploding with information all the time. With the constant stimuli and ever-expanding avenues and form factors, we are under constant stress to keep up. One way to manage **Information Anxiety** is to start with taming your e-mail and then expand the skills to other areas of life.

Let us look at the statistics of email and the effect it has on worker productivity. In 2013, the number of business emails sent and received per day totaled over 100 billion. This figure is expected to grow at an average annual rate of 7% over the next four years, reaching over 132 billion by the end of 2017. If you look at the volume of e-mail an average office worker receives, it has reached an average of about 109 email messages per day, according to a research by Radicati Group.[3]

More than a quarter (28%) of the average worker's day is spent answering and reading emails, according to a study by McKinsey Global Institute and International Data Corp.[4]

And it is difficult to return to work after checking email. In a recent study, a group of <u>Microsoft</u> workers took, on average, 15 minutes to return to serious mental tasks, like writing reports or computer code, after responding to incoming e-mail or instant messages.[5]

The common reaction to the arrival of an email is to react almost as quickly as responding to telephone calls. This means the interrupt effect is comparable with that of a telephone call.[6]

This book came about when I started to randomly poll my colleagues at Microsoft and others in the tech industry on how many hours a day they spent on email. The first answer was a big sigh. Followed by "gosh, I don't know." Then after another deep breath, the answer would be anywhere between three to six hours! It did not matter if the person was a program manager, a project manager, marketing manager, designer or in software development/test. The lowest end were software developers, for whom email was less important than their Visual Studio or other development environment tool they used. I did some quick math and figured out that if one were able to cut out one hour of email per day, the net productivity added would be 250 hours per year, or 6 weeks! If you calculate the number of employees for a typical Fortune 500 company and the average cost of a typical hour worked, you can quickly see the savings run into **millions of dollars per year**.

I developed this system and have practiced it for a couple of years now, and I can say it works well. I wrote the book in a format that is simple and easy to follow, and in a way that people can go through the first half of the book one time and set up the system for themselves. The second half, discipline, is the hardest and it is directly proportional to how much you are committed to addressing this issue.

Is this system perfect? It is certainly is a step in the right direction, and customizable to your circumstance. You will be able to discover your own "ideal" system by using some of the tips in this book.

As long you treat e-mail as *a* means of communication and not ***the*** means of communication, you will be fine.

One quick note - I designed my system on Microsoft Outlook®. If you don't use Microsoft Outlook® you will not benefit from this book/system as much. However, after years of trying several e-mail clients, I think Outlook® is *one of the best* systems, if used properly. It is my favorite for all my e-mail, whether at work or home.

E-mail Basics

Let us start with the e-mail basics. E-mail was created as a communication medium. I still recall the day I sent my first e-mail and received a reply back in a few minutes. The instantaneous communication and the immediate gratification surpassed any other mode of communication I had used till then. Eventually several other communication means evolved but the net of it still remained that ultimately e-mail is a means of communicating what is in your head to someone else with absolute clarity and highest fidelity and minimum interference. Somewhere along the way the e-mail volume exploded and managing e-mail became almost a full time job. I hope over the next few tips you put e-mail in perspective and are able to self-reflect with an intention of getting a handle on your e-mail overload.

1. E-mail is a means to an end

My whole attitude to email changed about six to seven years ago when I was talking to a classmate on one of my trips to India. My friend took the entrepreneurial route (and very successfully too) and has since built a multi-million dollar business that spans several countries. Over dinner we were comparing notes on everything and when talking about technology I mentioned the sheer volume of email. My friend said – "I would never be able to run a business if I spent that kind of time on email". Then he made a profound statement:

"Whenever you are replying to an email, you are doing someone else's work."

This was my Aha! moment. The more I thought about it the more it makes sense. Unless you are in customer support or your management chain is prolific at generating e-mail and expecting a response, that single statement should cut down your e-mail workload by about 25%.

I have another friend whose manager sent him 12 emails from 7:30 am to 9 am on a Sunday! We were meeting for breakfast when he showed me his phone and said "How do I deal with THIS?" We brainstormed and put in a custom "Manager Management plan" in place and one of the options on the plan was to look for another job!!

2. Consolidation

One of the first things you need to do is take an inventory of your email. A typical user may have up to four email accounts or even more.

1. Primary Personal e-mail account, e.g.: Hotmail.com or Outlook.com
2. Primary Work e-mail account
3. Secondary e-mail account, e.g.: Gmail, Yahoo
4. Spam e-mail account – an account you use when signing up for websites or other promotions where you have no intention of ever, ever using that email.

In addition to this there are sometimes additional e-mail accounts:

1. A home business account
2. A family email account to keep track of family calendars
3. An ISP-provided email account
4. Social/Charity related e-mail account

Similarly, you have multiple devices on which to check e-mail:
1. Work machine
2. Home Machine(s)
3. Smart Phone
4. Tablet

And soon you can visualize the proliferation of email accounts. So the first thing you need to do to manage email is to close unused accounts, and consolidate others.

In addition to this, I would encourage you to take inventory of your "collection points" of written notes, sticky notes, voicemail, Facebook, LinkedIn, Twitter, etc. - and soon you will notice that your whole communication landscape could use some consolidation.

3. Frequency

Another important aspect of e-mail management is to have fixed times in the day when you check email. The more often you check e-mail, the more likely you will be interrupted from the task at hand. Every email interruption takes away precious minutes to go back to the task at hand. Also, it is important to schedule your e-mail at times when you have a forced stop to end it. I always like to schedule my email primarily in three sessions:

- Before I leave for work
- Just before lunch
- After dinner, where I block out time to work on email that requires detailed responses.

Other times I walk around the office or use the phone and I am always available via instant messenger and mobile for anyone to reach me if needed. While your position may be required to check email more promptly, you may still be able to take advantage of this tip. Recently T Boone Pickens, the billionaire Oil investor, mentioned in an interview that good old conversation and phone beat any other productivity tool. You sure can't disagree with that.

4. Group E-mail Responses

Take a look at your mailbox and sort by Sender by sorting on the "Sent From" field. Then try to group the reply so that you are replying to one email vs. three. This is useful if you are replying to one person, and less useful if you are responding to an email conversation involving multiple people. This is best used with folks in your office who contribute the most volume of e-mail.

5. Better Subject Lines

Just writing a better email subject line makes an enormous difference. I can't emphasize this enough. This is the first step in writing successful email. Before you hit the Send button, PAUSE to think: "Who will read this? In what setting? How should they react to it?" Do you need an ACTION from them, or are you simply sharing information?

Once you send an email with a specific subject line, encourage people to stay on that topic throughout the email thread. If you see the topic begin to migrate, begin a new thread.

If you get a lot of email, so does everyone around you, and more so your managers. The typical rule of thumb I use is that every management level up gets about 35-50% more e-mail. The time required to respond to your email is even less, hence how one "Inspires Desire" to open and read your email is very important. Try to make subject line of interest to them, not just to you.

I have seen some teams use a consistent nomenclature by using the following acronyms to drive email communication efficiency. This works if everyone on the team follows these abbreviations:

AR: Action Required
HN: Help Needed
FYI: For Your Information
DNR: Do Not Reply
DNRA: Do Not Reply All
EOM: End of Message, used especially if the subject line serves as the entire message

6. Better E-mail Writing

This I must emphasize: Writing good email is hard. Writing good email consistently, in a world overflowing with information @ the speed of thought, is next to impossible. Some people are naturals. Others can be trained.

I would like to cite the example of Allison Watson, a Microsoft Corporate Vice President who runs the marketing for North America. She is a master at taking an extremely complex topic and netting out the content to the bare minimum of words with no loss in fidelity. In fact, after she has edited and approved a communication (an email, a presentation deck), you can look at the pre- and post-content and the light dawns.

In fact, her rigor and her bar are so high that she has mandated her entire team to go through a communication skills training, as she understands the impact it has on the organization. The rigor is required to ensure clarity in accountability and designed risks and outcomes. This enables speed of execution - despite what can sometime feel like a longer time to obsess over brevity.

Allison reminded me of this quote from President Woodrow Wilson.

A member of the Cabinet congratulated Wilson on introducing the vogue of short speeches and asked him about the time it took him to prepare his speeches. He said: "It depends. If I am to speak ten minutes, I need a week for preparation; if fifteen minutes, three days; if half an hour, two days; if an hour, I am ready now."

> ATTRIBUTION: President WOODROW WILSON.—Josephus Daniels, The Wilson Era; Years of War and After, 1917–1923, p. 624 (1946).

In email, it all starts with 'who is the audience' and 'what is the context'? What does each person on the email need to do? Is there clarity of thought?

One article I would encourage everyone to read is "Mastering Email Overload" – by Stever Robbins" © 2004 published in Harvard Business School Working Knowledge.

The following section template is excerpted with permission from "Tips for Mastering Email Overload" (c) 2004 by Stever Robbins (www.SteverRobbins.com/articles), first published in Harvard Business School Working Knowledge.

- Use a subject line to *summarize*, not *describe*

BAD SUBJECT:	GOOD SUBJECT:
Subject: Deadline discussion	Subject: Recommend we ship product April 16th

- Give your reader full context at the start of your message.
- When you copy lots of people mark out why each person should care.

BAD CC:	GOOD CC:
To: AH; RG; JB;JM;AN Subject: Product Launch Plan The Product launch plan is done. Please review it in the attached deck.	To: AH; RG; JB; JM; AN Subject: Product Launch Plan AN: DECISION NEEDED. Get marketing to approve the branding

	AH: PLEASE VERIFY. Does the slogan capture our branding?
	JM; RG; JB: FYI, if we need rebranding, your launch will slip.
	The Product launch plan is done. Please review it in the attached deck.

When scheduling a call or conference, include the topic in the invitation. It helps people prioritize and manage their calendar more effectively.

BAD E-MAIL:	GOOD E-MAIL:
Subject: Conference call Wednesday at 3:00 p.m.	Subject: Conference call Wednesday at 3:00 p.m. to review product launch presentation

E-mail Set up

In this section I will walk you through how to set up your primary machine to get most efficient on e-mail. I personally like to do ALL of my e-mail on 1 machine. The e-mail software I use is Outlook® 2013 and hence all the screenshots will use Outlook® 2013, though most tips would work for previous versions of Outlook® as well. The system involves three things

1. **Design and Delay** - Set up and design your system and introduce a conscious, deliberate delay, so you won't be an impulsive auto responder to *every e-mail*
2. **Discipline** - Once you have set up your system, you can now enforce discipline. Start small, with 30-minute increments, till you find a system that is optimum for you.
3. **Delegation** - This is how you delegate the work to more efficiently handle e-mail.

Below is the visual that should help you get going.

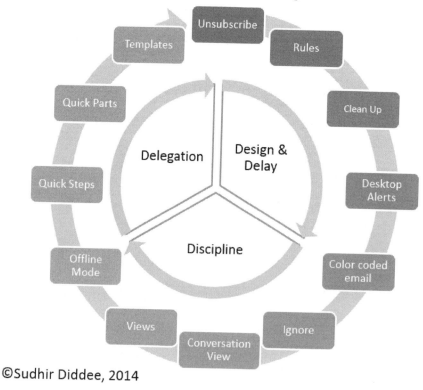

Figure 1

8

Design and Delay

Now, before you even read any further, pause and answer this question honestly: Have you ever purposefully looked at your email system? In most cases the answer will be no, or never thought of it. We join a new work place and we are assigned a machine, we fire up Outlook® and start using it. Over a period of time we create folders, add a few rules, join a few distribution lists and before we know it, we are consumed by email. In this section we will talk about taking time to very thoughtfully design the system.

Take a blank piece of paper and make three columns. In the first column define your five to seven key priorities for the year. In the next, write down five to ten key stakeholders you work with. In the last column, take an inventory of your e-mail and write down where you see the most email volume by subject and contact. Now, compare and see if it aligns to the first two columns. If not, the following section should help you design your email system. Let us then get going and set up your Outlook® the right way.

7. Default Tab

The first thing in the setup is to change the default tab from Inbox to Tasks. The reason: everything you do should be a Task aligned to your goals. The goals should be logical, whether for business, personal, financial etc.

To change the default tab, use the following Steps:

Step 1 – Go to File, Options, Advanced, Outlook start and exit

Step 2 – Click **Browse** and select **Task**

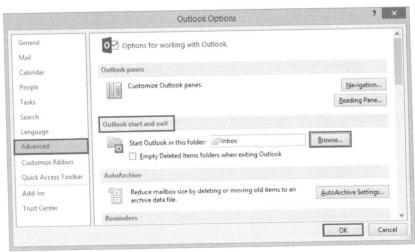

Figure 2

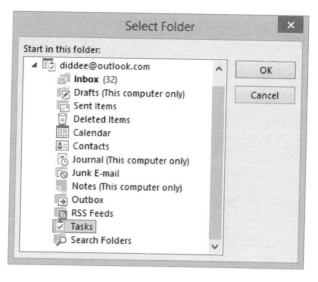

Figure 3

Now when you open Outlook® next time, you will start in Tasks. I recommend transferring all your tasks into Outlook® and create tasks quickly by typing **CTRL+SHIFT+K** to build on the task list.

8. Unsubscribe

This tip comes straight from an interview with Steve Ballmer, the legendary former Microsoft CEO. He mentioned to the interviewer that he shares his email address at every speech. When the interviewer asked him how he managed his email, his answer was very candid:

*"...why do people get a lot of mail? They get a lot of mail, **because they sign up to get a lot of mail**, because they get spammed by a lot of mail, but people don't waste other people's time, generally."* [7]

The more I thought about it and pondered over it the more it made sense.

Hence once of the most important rules of e-mail set up is to unsubscribe from every email list, alerts, newsletters, deals that you don't want. And don't drop your business card at the local diner or a trade show to enter a drawing, or you will be inviting more mail.

One other piece of advice is to unsubscribe from one email list per day. Over a year you will end up unsubscribing from all e-mail lists and you will be very, very careful about giving your email address anywhere.

9. Turn off unnecessary alerts

One of the volume generators for email is all the social networks and their e-mail alerts. It wouldn't surprise me if the biggest volume of traffic is generated for the social networks by their e-mail alerts. It is no surprise that in almost every social network it is extremely tricky to turn off the e-mail notification, which is checked to allow alerts by default.

We are all human and whenever there is a new picture posted the curiosity gets better of most individuals and you end up logging in to see what is new. Before you realize, you have lost a good part of the hour doing something totally unrelated. If you can take care of alerts for Facebook, Twitter, GroupOn and LinkedIn you should be on your way to managing email.

One of the hardest things to figure out is how to turn off the alerts in the social networks. If you look at the addictiveness of social networks, they are built off of e-mail. If LinkedIn sends you an email that one of your contacts has a new job, the natural tendency is to click and check this out, but this is outside the time you may have set for social networks. Hence my advice – **TURN OFF ALL ALERTS** and non-essential e-mails.

In any case, I believe you are always in touch with your best contacts, friends, and family whether or not social networks exist. Some of my best mentors and managers are not on any of my networks since I make it a point to meet with them or call them regularly.

10. Rules

We have established that one of the biggest problems people face is e-mail overload. However, most of the e-mail can be easily managed by setting rules, where e-mails from certain people or teams can go directly into a particular folder. For example, e-mails from your manager can be routed into a separate folder. E-mails sent to you where you are in the "cc line" (instead of in the more action-oriented "to" line) can go to a different folder, or your e-mail stock alerts can go to your investing folder.

Here are the steps to create rules:

Step 1 - Click on **Rules** under the Home Tab

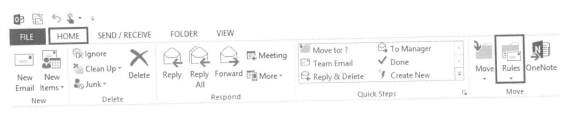

Figure 4

Step 2 - Click on the e-mail for which you want to create a new rule and click on **Create Rule** (In this case we are creating a rule for MarketWatch© Alerts.)

Figure 5

Step 3 – You will see the rule conditions

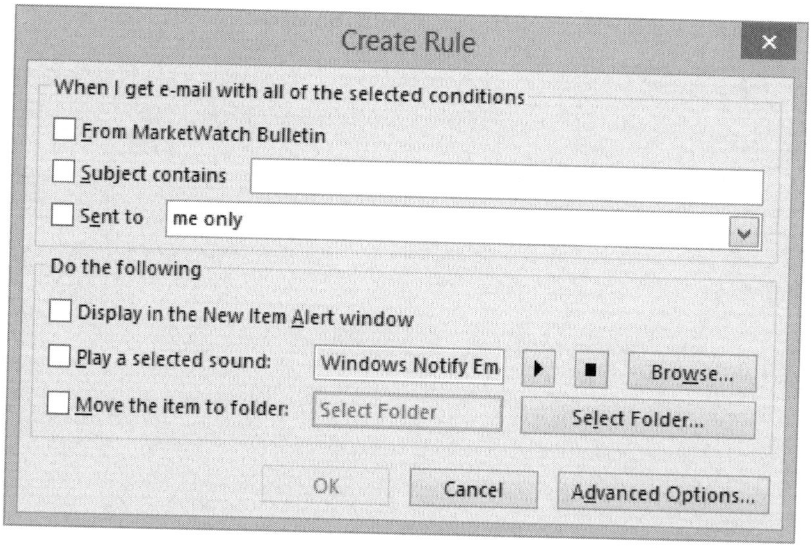

Figure 6

Step 4 - Select the conditions for the **Move to MarketWatch Folder** rule

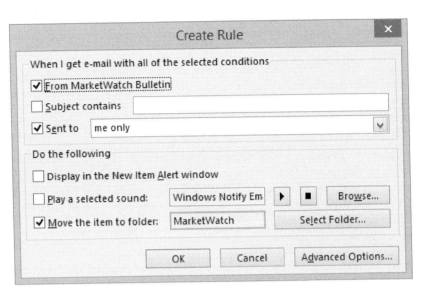

Figure 7

Now, all future emails from MarketWatch will go into a new MarketWatch folder. Alternatively you can always create a rule on the fly by right-clicking a message. Just select MOVE to move the emails on a project to their respective project folder if your preference is to always organize communication by projects.

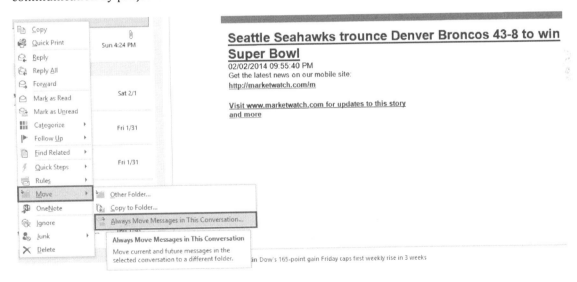

Figure 8

11. Desktop Alerts

Desktop alerts have a purpose to alert you if a new email has just come in. This is very handy, especially if you are in a critical project and sequential work or updates control the next step in the workflow. However, for the majority of information workers, you can safely turn off this one distraction that is in your control. If you are not the one to be distracted by alerts then you can let it be, but the additional advantage of turning off alerts is, when sharing a desktop or presenting at a meeting, your e-mail alerts don't turn into an inadvertent embarrassment for you.

Step 1 – Go to **File, Options**

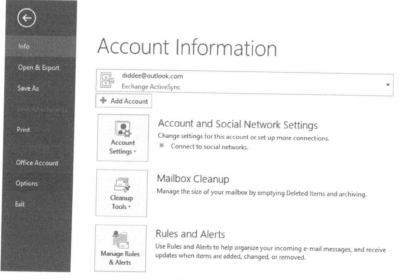

Figure 9

Step 2 – Click on Mail and scroll down till you find **Message Arrival** (under Mail) and **uncheck** the box – "Display a Desktop Alert". Note, alerts are extremely useful when used correctly, but more often than not it is difficult to focus if you keep getting pop ups about new email.

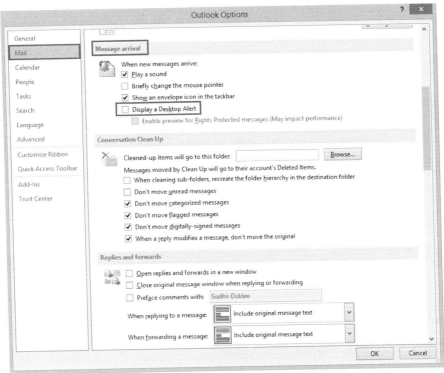

Figure 10

Now you have a trifle more control on your attention span. ☺

12.Preview Reading Pane

One useful option in Outlook® is the reading pane. This is helpful if you configure it to suit your needs. It is useful if much of the email you receive is information-centric, or perhaps you need to see it but not read it in depth. This serves to quickly let you know if you can delete the email.

Figure 11

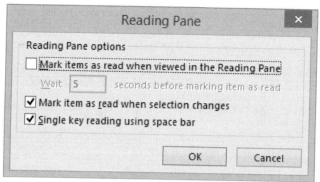

Figure 12

13. Color Coding E-mail

Color coding your email can help you save time to visually sort your mailbox by using colors. To make your manager's e-mails to you pop, have them automatically appear in red text. E-mails which are sent only to you can appear in blue text. E-mails sent to a group you belong to, e.g.: Weekend Cyclists, can appear in purple, and so on.

To customize and view your e-mail by color in Microsoft Outlook® 2010 here the steps:

If your inbox looks like this:

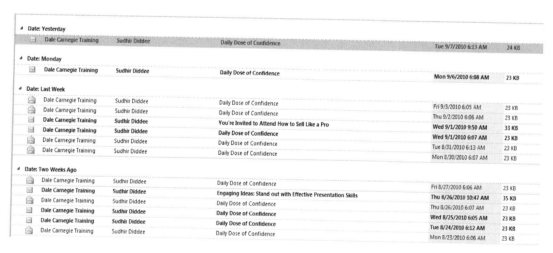

Figure 13

And you want your inspirational e-mails from the mailing list "Daily Dose of Confidence" to appear in Green, here are the steps:

Step 1 - Click on **View, View Settings**

Figure 14

Step 2 - Click on **Conditional Formatting**

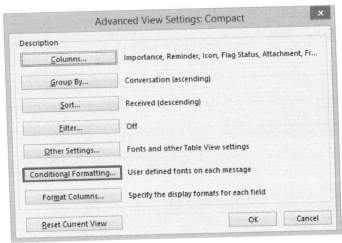

Figure 15

Step 3 - Click on **Add**

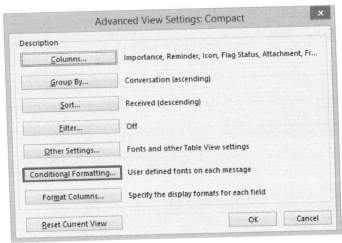

Figure 16

Step 4 - Click on **Condition**

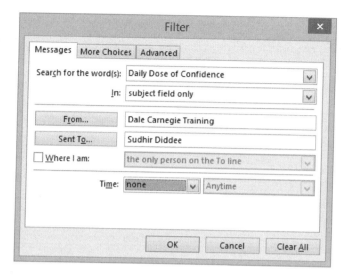

Figure 17

Step 5- Click on **Font,** assign a unique font and color and click **OK**

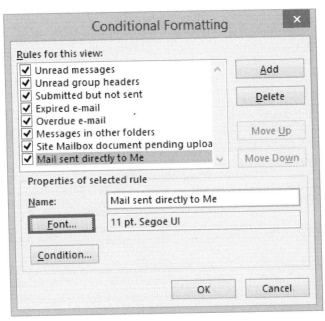

Figure 18

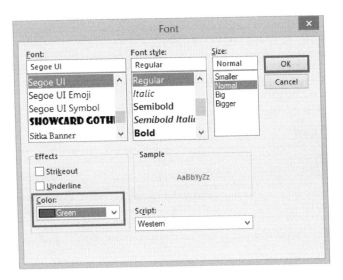

Figure 19

Step 6 - Click **OK** and exit the window

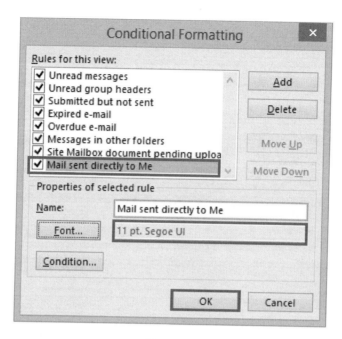

Figure 20

Step 7 - Your e-mail view will change. My Daily Dose of Confidence e-mails will now appear in **GREEN**

Figure 21

14.Signature

Whether you run a small business or are in a big company, it is always a good idea to include a signature with your contact information at the end of your email. You can create a unique signature for your each of your email accounts, or choose between different signatures for a single account. To create a signature, follow these steps.

Step 1 – Go to File, Options

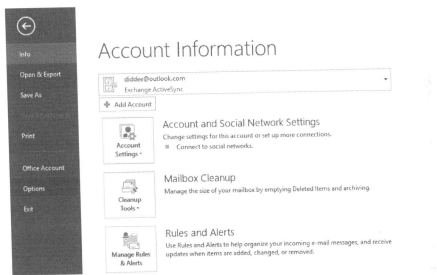

Figure 22

Step 2 – Go to **Mail**, **Compose Messages**, **Signatures**

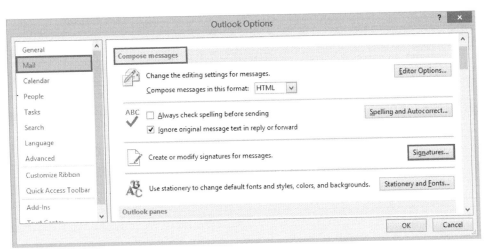

Figure 23

Step 3 – Select the E-Mail account and **Click New**

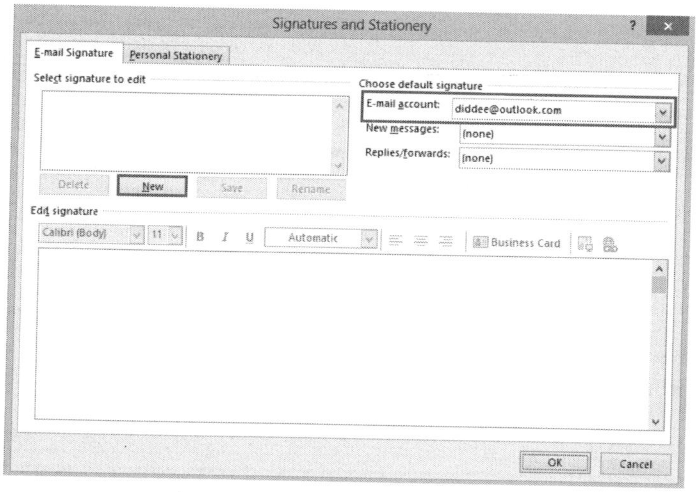

Figure 24

Step 4 – Give Name to the signature

Figure 25

Step 5 – Type in the Signature in Edit signature section and click **OK**

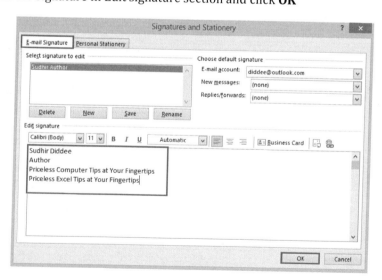

Figure 26

Step 6 – Click **OK** as shown in the figure below.

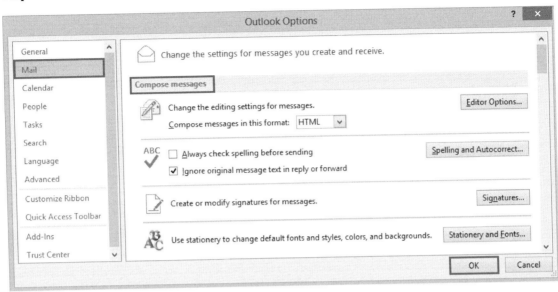

Figure 27

Next time you create a new email, your signature will appear automatically as shown below. While you can also show your full signature on each follow-up message, it is best to have it appear only on new messages.

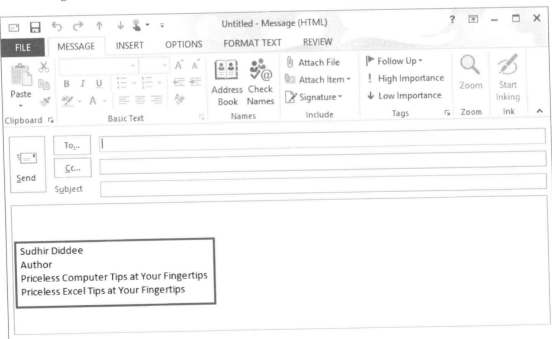

Figure 28

15. E-mail Folders

This is for the highly organized, compulsive filers. One of the most effective ways for people to improve their productivity on email, particularly if you are the systematic kind, is to make sure your folder management across your key folders are identical. The key sets are:

- Email folders
- PC folders
  - I have all my desktop/laptop folders synchronized to OneDrive (www.onedrive.com) so that I have a consistent folder structure at my work and home machines.
- Internet browser folders
- Archive mail folders

This way all emails/documents and web links are always in synch and related information is found at the same place across various collection points.

Note: this may be hard to do, but once done, the information retrieval becomes really easy.

16. Linked Mail Boxes

This command can save time in your day-to-day work and improve productivity, especially with multiple mail boxes. With Outlook® you can have multiple mail boxes linked to the same Outlook® client (as long as POP email is supported on your mail account). So when you have to send email you don't have to log into various websites – just synch and you are set.

Similarly, you can send email from any account by just clicking on the down arrow and choosing the email account from which you want to send the particular email. Some companies allow users to have both work and personal email on work computer, particularly if your company has the policy of BYOC (Bring Your Own Computer). If your company allows that then you can configure all your email accounts on the same Outlook® client and choose the email to use when sending email.

Here is how it works. In the example below the default email is book@vyanjan.com. If I want to change it to diddee@vyanjan.com or sudhirdiddee@vyanjan.com then I can click on the down arrow and select the email I want.

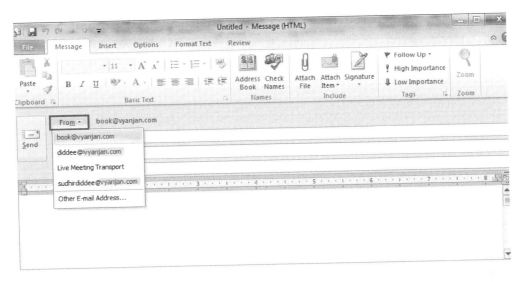

Figure 29

To set up multiple emails accounts on the same Outlook® client just go to **File, Info, Add Account** and follow the steps. The steps are really straightforward and you will be up and running in no time.

Figure 30

A similar option exists on most smart phones (Windows Phones and iPhones) to consolidate email.

Discipline in E-mail Management

The next and the **most important** rule in e-mail management is discipline. If you look at some of the most efficient people in the company it will be the senior leaders of the company. Their time is not their time as it is decided by the priorities of the company and they have to show up. Be it a customer meeting, employee recruiting event, etc., their time is booked solidly and they go from meeting to meeting. A good portion of their time is invested in people development, which affords them little time to be on email. Hence they usually get e-mail discipline by design in terms of their work. You, however, may have to consciously build a discipline - and soon you will be given more to handle and you will then find yourself in the leadership of your company where these skills will come in very handy!

The following tips are how to get through your email more efficiently.

17.Conversation Clean Up

If you are away from your computer for a while, say 4-6 hours or more, you are weighed down at the back of your mind by the number of unread emails awaiting you upon your return. One of the most dreaded feelings of anyone coming back from even one week's vacation is the thought of finding 1000+ unread messages. The only ways I have seen people take care of it is – either spend 2-4 hours catching up on email the day before they return to work, or spend half a day on the first day back at work just dealing with email. So, many folks use Out of Office messages to inform others that they are "catching up on email," which, while reasonable, is simply an inefficient use of time.

As you develop your new system and get comfortable using it, you should introduce yourself to the Conversation Clean Up feature in Outlook®, first introduced in Outlook® 2010. Conversation Clean Up, simply stated, cleans up all redundant threads of a conversation. So, for example, if someone started a thread on "Top support issues blocking sales" and there were 15 responses – you don't need to read 15 emails on the topic. If you run Clean Up, it will clean all the threads **while preserving those that have an attachment.**

You can significantly reduce the number of messages in your mail folders by using the Conversation Clean Up feature in Microsoft Outlook® 2013 (and 2010). Redundant messages throughout a Conversation will be moved to the Deleted Items folder.

Conversation Clean Up is most useful on Conversations with many responses back and forth especially with many recipients.

Figure 31

You can choose to Clean Up either the entire Folder or just the conversation. If you click on the drop down you will have the following options

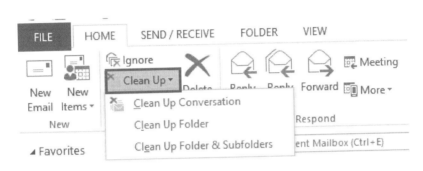

Figure 32

Clean Up Conversation   The current Conversation is reviewed, and redundant messages are deleted. Best used on a daily basis

Clean Up Folder   All Conversations in the selected folder are reviewed, and redundant messages are deleted. Best used at the start of the day or after a vacation.

Clean Up Folder & Subfolders   All Conversations in the selected folder and any folder that it contains are reviewed, and redundant messages are deleted. Ideally used when you want a through clean-up of your email.

18.Ignore

This is one of the best features of Microsoft Outlook® which was first introduced in Outlook® 2010. It does require Microsoft Exchange Server® 2010, but is very useful if you find yourself on an e-mail thread you don't want to be on. Let's say you were added to your office's sports fantasy league. This is not your personal passion, and the number of e-mails is overwhelming. Just click the **Ignore button** while on any e-mail of that thread. The Ignore button quickly and easily moves an entire conversation -- *and* any <u>future</u> items that arrive -- to your Deleted Items folder.

Figure 33

Even though this feature is in plain sight, most of the users are unaware of this powerful feature.

19.Views

Views are one of the best features of Microsoft Outlook® 2010. You can have preconfigured views if you quickly want to see certain filters.

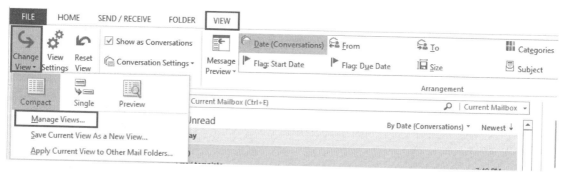

Figure 34

For example, some people want to start the day viewing only unread e-mail.

Click on **Change View** to select

- Views which show only high importance (!)
- View of e-mails from your manager and/or management chain
- A weekend view where only certain messages are filtered through
- By categories, etc. You can create custom views based on your unique needs.

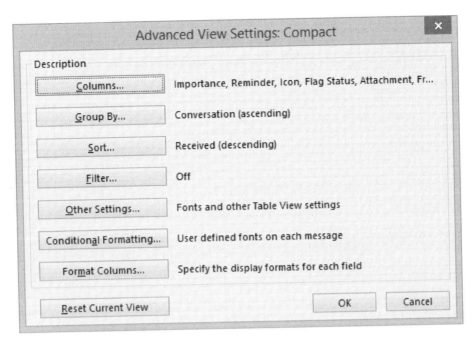

Figure 35

20.Conversation View

One of the common complaints of users is to find an inbox full of messages, several of which relate to the same conversation. If you switch on the **Conversation View**, all your e-mails are grouped into conversations based on the subject of the e-mail. This is especially helpful on your first morning back from a two-week vacation. To turn on the **Conversation View**, follow these steps:

Step 1 - Go to **View** and Check the box **Show as Conversations**.

Figure 36

Step 2 - Select the appropriate folder when prompted.

Figure 37

Step 3 - All of your e-mails appear as conversations.

If you expand a conversation, you can see all related messages, including your replies from your Sent Items. The software is so slick that it even tracks who replied to someone else. You should definitely try it; it is likely you will get an immediate productivity boost in your e-mail handling.

21. Pull vs. Push Synchronization

The smartphones have literally put the internet in our pockets. With that there is frictionless access to applications and e-mails 24 x 7. I have polled friends and co-workers and everyone has admitted that whenever they are woken up from their sleep they have a tendency to check e-mail, or worse, as they are trying to go to sleep and there is a familiar buzz to tell them of an incoming e-mail, they take a sneak peek to see who sent the e-mail.

One way to work around this is to set all your e-mails to "Pull vs. Push" email. By Pull I mean going into settings and changing the synchronization settings to Synchronize manually. You can change the settings to every hour, every day etc. As long as you have it set to anything other than 'as they arrive', you will go a long way from being interrupted by e-mail. All my e-mail is set to manually synch. Unless I am expecting an important email or a notification (e.g. an e-mail notifying me of the delivery of my passport, or at critical times of the year like fiscal year milestones etc.), I set my e-mail to manually synch once a day at the gym while on the treadmill.

On my phone for the work email, I just synch my calendar and not the email unless I am on the road.

This is almost akin to the surface of a lake where constant pebbles are being thrown at regular intervals. The water never gets to settle. Constantly incoming e-mails are the pebbles which tend to clutter our work time and get in the way of us clearly seeing the priorities at work for the day.

MICROSOFT SETTINGS

Account name

Microsoft

Download new content

as items arrive

every 15 minutes

every 30 minutes

hourly

manually

Download email from

the last 7 days

Figure 38

You can take the setting to the next level by only synching your calendar, contacts and tasks. This setting works wonders, except when you are trying to send a quick e-mail in response to a meeting; e.g.: to let the attendees know your current meeting is running over, or you are stuck in traffic. If you don't synch your e-mail then the notification will be sent using your other account on the phone, which could be your personal account. That might be fine, except that some e-mails might be treated as spam and end up in the junk folder. Something to be aware of when not synching your work e-mail.

MICROSOFT SETTINGS

Download new content

manually

Download email from

the last 7 days

Content to sync

☐ Email

☑ Contacts

☑ Calendar

☑ Tasks

Figure 39

The other advantage of this setting is that you give up your membership of the "**Heads Down Tribe;**" people who are obsessively heads down on their phone in elevators, hallways, bus lines, parking lots etc.

23.Work in Offline Mode

Once your scheduled time on e-mail is over, here is the best thing you can do to add to your productivity – work on Outlook® in Offline mode. This means that all of your information on Outlook® is available, but it is not updated real-time. The plus: you are not distracted by incoming email and you can give your full, undivided attention to the task/meeting at hand. The flip side is that you cannot send e-mail either. Hence, you may be replying to a thread that someone else may have already replied to. It requires a bit of practice; e.g.: don't go in Offline mode in the mornings or late afternoon when the email activity is high or when you are expecting an important e-mail. It will require a bit of practice, but over time you can use it very effectively.

To go in Offline mode, follow the steps in the screenshot below. Go to **Send/Receive, Work Offline:**

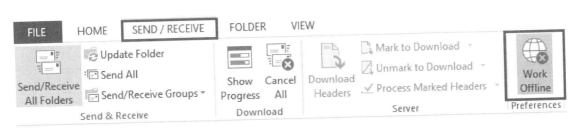

Figure 40

The button appears highlighted and Outlook® tells you that you are working offline in the status bar. And the status bar shows this message:

Figure 41

E-mail Delegation

The last part of the e-mail overload management process is delegation. You may think to yourself, "but I have no-one to delegate things to." Delegation is broadly used to include delegating to the right people, delegating to the software to do repeatable tasks for you, and delegating to yourself by **deferring** it to work on at a future time marked on the calendar.

24.Quick Steps

Quick Steps are a life-saver if you want to file e-mail or need to send e-mails to the same group. Quick Steps evolve as you go through various projects to suit specific needs.

Some Quick Steps are created automatically for you by Microsoft Outlook®, and you can also create some to meet your needs. I have one for Order Confirmation for all my online purchases. I also have one for tracking all summer camp information for my kids. At the end of the summer, I might delete the Summer Camp Quick Step and replace it with School Work or something else.

Let's say I am planning a vacation to Turkey. There will be a lot of planning from research, tips from friends, tickets and hotels. In order to track everything, I create a folder called Vacation Turkey. I want to put all my e-mail into this folder to file the trip related e-mails away with a single click from the ribbon vs. trying to copy each e-mail item into the new folder that I created as it arrives while I plan my trip.

Here are the steps to create a Quickstep.

Step 1 - Locate Quick Steps under the Microsoft Outlook® Ribbon and select **Create New**

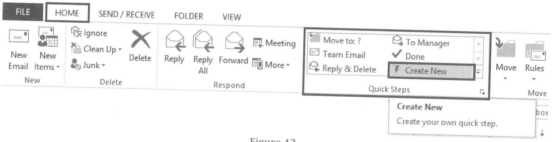

Figure 42

34

Step 2 - Select Move to Folder and change status to Mark as Read

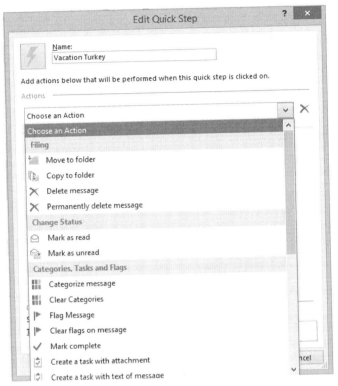

Figure 43

Step 3 - Choose the Folder

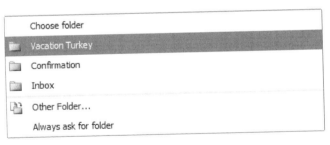

Figure 44

Step 4 – Select **Finish** under Edit Quick Step

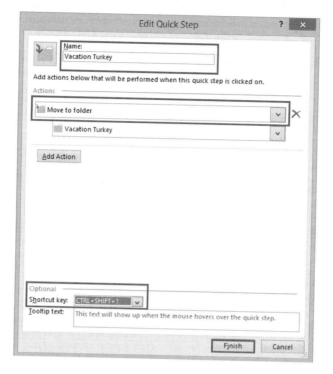

Figure 45

There are some smart scenarios built into the default Microsoft Outlook®, and the Outlook® team has done an excellent job on this. Some of the common prebuilt Quick Step scenarios are:

Meeting Reply – Some conversations on e-mail can get too long or may only be solved by scheduling a meeting. Just click on Meeting Reply and all the people on the thread get automatically added to the meeting.
To Manager – If you need to send an e-mail to your manager, this Quick Step is useful.
Team E-mail –If you need to distribute some information to your team, Team E-mail Quick Steps comes in handy.
Team Meeting – Useful for setting meetings with a team or group.

There are two steps to go to a Quick Step folder. You can hold down the Control key while clicking on the Quick Step to navigate to the folder:

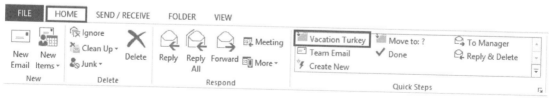

Figure 46

Or right-click on any Quick Step which has an associated option to either navigate to that folder or work with the Quick Step, including duplicating and adding to Quick Access Toolbar

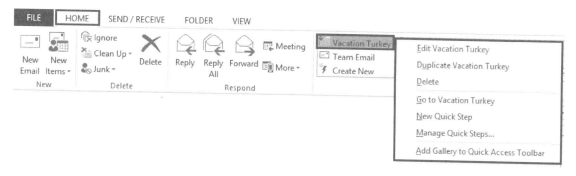

Figure 47

25. Quick Parts

Quick Parts is a lifesaver if you constantly find yourself typing the same text over and over again. You may know that you can set up signatures to quickly insert into an email (look for Signature on the Text tab of the **Insert** ribbon). Quick Parts is like a signature that you can insert anywhere in an e-mail. For example, say you are often asked for directions to your office. Instead of cutting and pasting (or worse, retyping) all the time, you can type in "Here is the address", hit the **Enter key**, and the auto-text that you have set up will insert the directions. Other ideas for use of Quick Parts are inserting a list of resources you frequently need to send to people you work with on projects, internal and external site references etc. Quick Parts can save you a lot of time.

Here are the steps:

Step 1 - Create a new e-mail message.
Step 2 - Type in the text that you want to use as a **Quick Part**.
Step 3 - Highlight the text and select **Quick Parts** from the Text tab of the **Insert** ribbon.

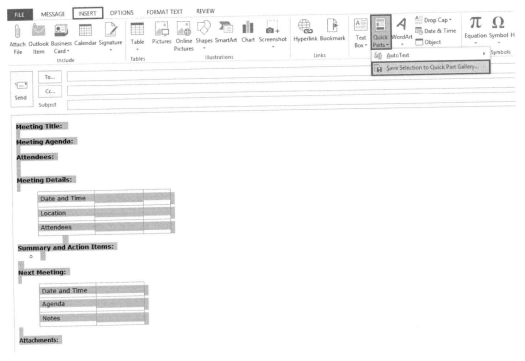

Figure 48

Step 4 - Click on **Save Selection to Quick Part Gallery**.
Step 5 - Give it a name and enter the **Category** and **Options**. And you're done!

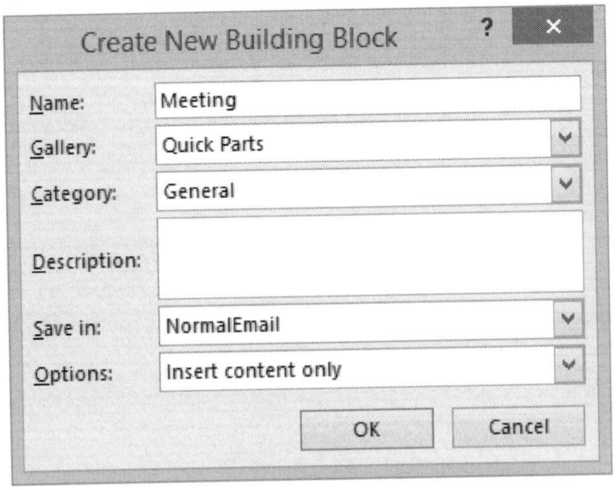

Figure 49

Next time you create a document, just type in the name of the Quick Part and it will appear where the cursor is blinking. Hit **Enter**.

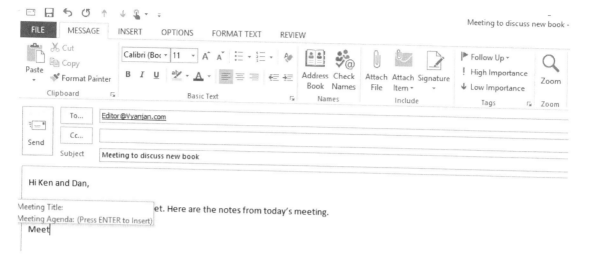

Figure 50

Here is how it appears:

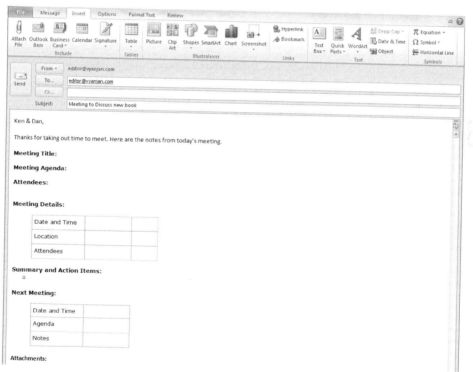

Figure 51

26. Quick Access Toolbar

Quick Access Toolbar allows you to access most commonly used functions. I love to have the Work Offline and Close All Items in the Quick Access Toolbar. This allows me to quickly switch between Offline and online mode. Also I have Close All Items which is useful when I want to de-clutter my desktop and close all open emails but not close Outlook®.

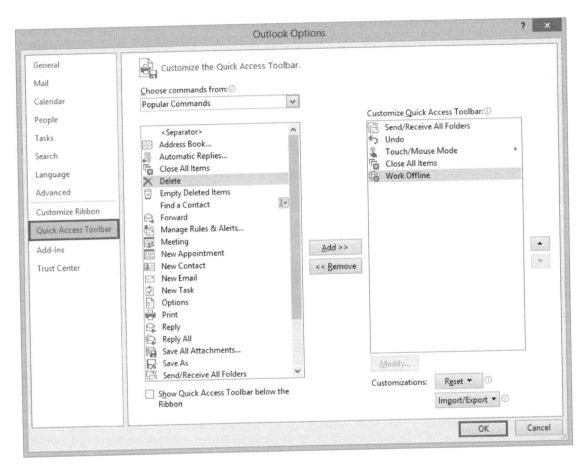

Figure 52

27. Instant Search and Features

If you are using Microsoft Outlook® Instant Search often, just type in **CTRL+E** to quickly get to the Instant Search box.

As the e-mail load increases for information workers, more and more information is stored in Microsoft Outlook® and it has become the default document repository. Search E-mail has become a life saver, but here are some tricks which will take this feature to a whole new level.

This is a simple search example where I search for "MarketWatch." All the e-mails with the term "MarketWatch" are returned, with the search term highlighted.

Figure 53

The senders are MarketWatch Bulletin, MarketWatch e-Newsletter, and MarketWatch Alerts. The number of items is listed in a status bar. In this case we have 151 items and these results are not very useful.

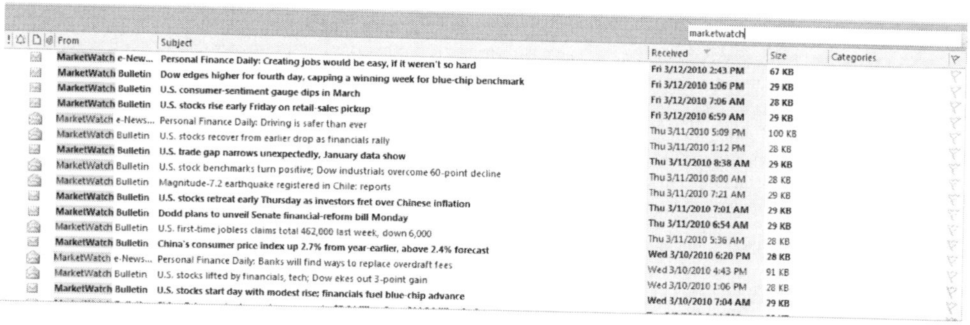

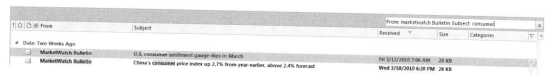

Figure 54

Let's say you were searching for an e-mail that you recall was sent by MarketWatch Bulletin, and had a subject line which mentioned consumer sentiment. There are steps to quickly get to the e-mail. Enter the following in the Search Box, and watch your lost email magically appear:

From: MarketWatch Bulletin Subject: consumer

Figure 55

Or, let's assume someone sent you an e-mail with a Microsoft PowerPoint® attachment. You can quickly get to that e-mail by typing the following string:

From: Person's Name **Attach:*.pptx**

Example: From: Sailesh Attach:*pptx ; or From: Sujaya Attach:*.docx

It will return all e-mails from that person with a Microsoft PowerPoint attachment (or other file types).

You can also use: **hasattachments: yes**

Figure 56

You can configure the search options by going to **File**, **Options, Search.** You can define the Scope, Refine Search criteria like From, Subject, Categorized, Where it was sent this week, Importance etc.

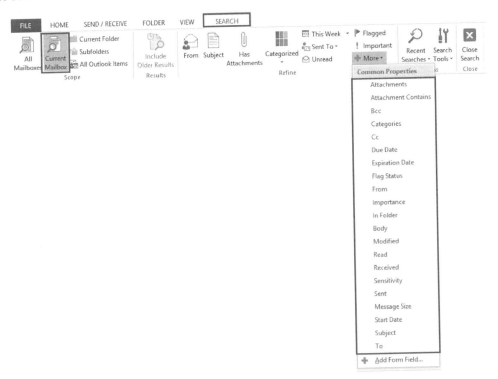

Figure 57

28.Replies "Direct Replies To" feature

If you are sending a message that requires a response that other people must also receive, use the **"Direct Replies To"** feature. This ensures that when each recipient clicks on reply, all of the applicable addresses will automatically be in the "To" field, eliminating both the reliance on the recipient to remember to select "Reply all" and the extra time you may need to spend on forwarding the replies.

Step 1 - On a new message click on **Direct Replies To**

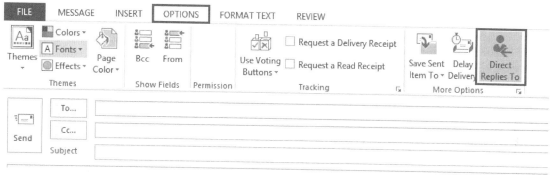

Figure 58

Step 2 - Check the box **Have replies sent to** under delivery options.

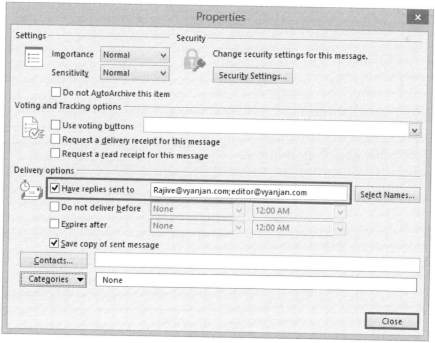

Figure 59

29. E-mail Templates

Let's say you have a standard template for monthly reports, meeting minutes or for project management status updates. Instead of creating a new e-mail and copying from a Microsoft Word document, you can use e-mail templates. You would create your template once, and from then on you can modify the relevant sections.

Here is how it works:

Step 1 - Create a new e-mail message
Step 2 - Enter e-mail addresses of regular recipients
Step 3 - Enter the text, in this case the "Meeting Minutes" template

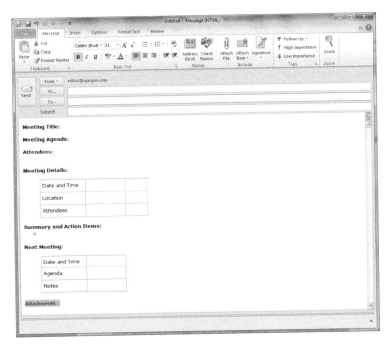

Figure 60

Step 4 - Click on **File – Save As**

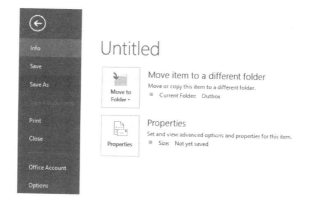

Figure 61

Step 5 - In the drop down menu, select **Outlook® Template**

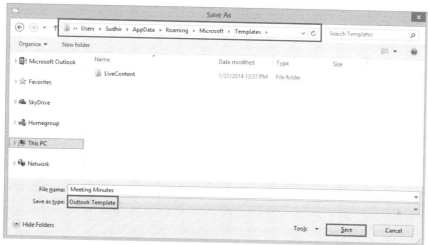

Figure 62

Step 6 - Give the name to the template, and click **Save**

Your template is saved in this directory by default:

C:\Users\USER NAME\AppData\Roaming\Microsoft\Templates

You can change the directory structure to any directory you want.

To create a new e-mail using your template, follow these steps:

Step 1 - Click **File**, **Open**
Step 2 - Browse to the template directory (or to where you saved your template) usually
c:\users\username\appdata\roaming\microsoft\templates
Step 3 - Open the template, change anything you need to change and you're all set.

E-mail Best Practices

Here are some e-mail best practices or "Power Tips". I strongly urge you to spend time in this section and deliberately try to incorporate 5 to 10 of these tips in your daily work life. I try to apply *most* of these all the time and I can't tell you how delighted I am when I benefit from these tips. I do sincerely hope you as the reader try these and start benefiting from them straight away.

30. Send to OneNote®

OneNote® is one of my favorite Microsoft products, especially for organizing information. If you have not been exposed to OneNote®, just try it or send me an email and I will get you started. For most people Outlook® has become the universal information repository. One common excuse I hear from people having Outlook® open 10 hours a day is ..."All my information is in Outlook®". While I cannot disagree with this fact, one of the cool features is its seamless integration with OneNote®. On a typical day an average Office worker receives about 100 emails. If you are in a senior role, the email volume could be up to 200 emails a day. However, only 2-4% of the emails have content you need to refer to; e.g.: links to internal reporting sites, new policies that you may need to refer to or good emails you need to refer back to.

So, all you need to do is move those to OneNote®. And in any given year you will have only about 500 pages max of a notebook in OneNote. You can maintain one notebook per year. For example, when I received my billing statement for renewal of my MSDN subscription, I just moved it to OneNote as a proof of the payment confirmation.

Figure 63

In case you need to reuse the material – no need to cut and paste the content back into email. Just open the page in OneNote and press CTRL+SHIFT+E to mail the page to the recipient. This kind of seamless integration makes the Office suite enabled productivity priceless.

31.Change e-mail subject line

Since Outlook® has become the default collection point for all information, you can save an email by changing the subject line of an email locally for your reference.

One of the reasons people spend a lot time on emails is that often an email starts with something innocuous and soon morphs into something very serious. However, when looking through the old emails, you spend a lot of time finding the right email. To start to contribute to a better email system: whenever you see an email thread morphing, change the subject line to a more appropriate subject. Hence an email that started with a subject line "How was the weekend?" and turned into the projected growth of smartphones in Asia, you can change the final email subject using the following steps.

Step 1 – Double click to open the email in **Microsoft Outlook®**.

Step 2 – To change the subject line select (highlight) the subject line and just start typing in the subject line with text that will make the email more relevant to you

Step 3 – Go to **File**, **Save**

Now your email should be saved with the new subject.

32.Meeting Notes in OneNote®

Since this book is all about managing e-mail overload then let us start with meeting notes. With every meeting you attend, if you capture notes you would like to record the key points in addition to agenda, attendees, date and place. Fortunately one little button in the meeting invite makes it really easy. (This tip assumes you have OneNote installed.)

Step 1 – Click on **Meeting, Meeting Notes**

Figure 64

You will be prompted to choose between one of the options. Select Take notes on your own.

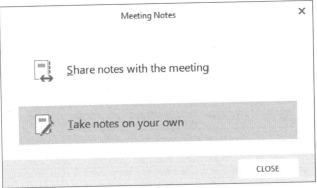

Figure 65

Step 2 – Choose which notebook you want to file the notes in.

Figure 66

Step 3- OneNote creates a page complete with Meeting Date, Location, a link to the Outlook® item, the participants etc. You can type the notes and save them effortlessly.

Figure 67

Step 4 - If you need to share your notes with the meeting participants, compose an e-mail by clicking **CTRL+SHIFT+E.** Note: all the participants are already in the To field.

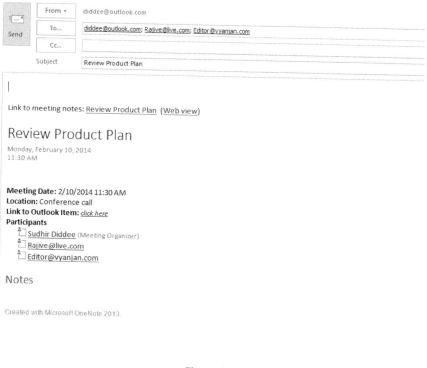

Figure 68

33.Writing for Smartphones

As smart phones have become ubiquitous, so has our consumption of email. In a recent article on the website eMarketer.com, the December 2013 data from **Return Path** highlighted this trend, showing that **more than half** of email "opens" worldwide **took place on mobile devices** during this past holiday season. The other two devices studied, desktops and webmail, came in at just around one-quarter of email opens each.

(Read more at http://www.emarketer.com/Article/Mobile-Email-Opens-Trump-Those-on-Desktop/1010526#lmESDbfFjPdrVTPl.99)

This underscores the importance of writing concise email or email specifically targeted at smart phone users. In fact, several studies have shown that email is the last thing people check before sleeping and the first thing on getting up. I know for a fact that several executives I have worked with regularly check their email around 5:30 am; hence the importance of writing crisp, concise email formatted for a smart phone.

A colleague of mine had significant success with field sellers when he started writing email formatted specially for smart phones. The idea is simple: cut out all graphics or banners in your email. Focus on the inverted-pyramid style of writing used in journalism and write the gist of your email at the top. If it is an important email, try sending it first to yourself and see how it reads in the most common formats of smart phones and what changes you need to make to get the user to scroll down or reply back. Make it enticing to engage with you.

34.Create Tasks Quickly

Tasks are a great way to plan your workday, and if you start planning your work around tasks versus Email, you will notice a distinct improvement in your personal productivity. If you see any email that has an action item for you, just create a task and then block time daily to go through the tasks.

To quickly create a new task, press **CTRL+SHIFT+K**. A new Task window will open.

One advantage of tasks is that you see the tangible output of your work. By moving completed tasks into folders categorized by Month or Year you can go back and see what you have been accomplishing. This is very useful at review time. I always like to check back once a month to ensure I am working on the most impactful tasks. If my tasks don't align with the success of the department and aren't likely to in the future, , it is perhaps time to have a conversation with my manager or to find another job that is more meaningful.

35. E-mail Tracking

Often when we send a critically important email, we are anxious as to whether the person we sent it to has received and read the email or not. Luckily for us, Outlook® has a built-in feature.

Step 1 – Compose the email as normal

Step 2 – Click on **Options, Tracking, and** you will see two boxes. Check both boxes if you want both Delivery Receipt and Read Receipt

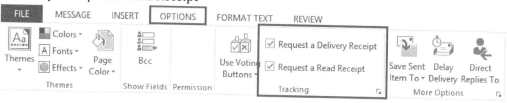

Figure 69

More options

If you want more options, click on the small arrow and the Tracking pop-up window opens

Figure 70

The pop up window looks like this. Select the options you want for the message. Try various options and you will have discovered a whole new way to manage the response options.

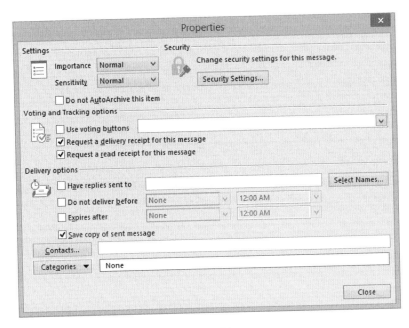

Figure 71

36. Open Next message immediately

When you delete an email, many times it will return you to the Inbox. Wouldn't it be faster to simply go to the next email? Follow these steps:

Step 1 - Launch **Microsoft Outlook**®. Go to the top and click **File**:

Step 2 - Click on the **Options** button:

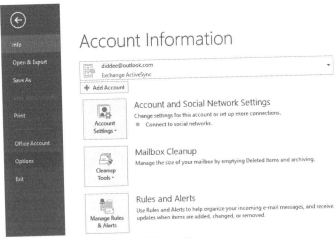

Figure 72

Step 3 - In the left pane, select **Mail**.

Step 4 - In the right pane, scroll down to the **other** section and in the section – **After moving and deleting an item** - set the drop down to **open the next item**

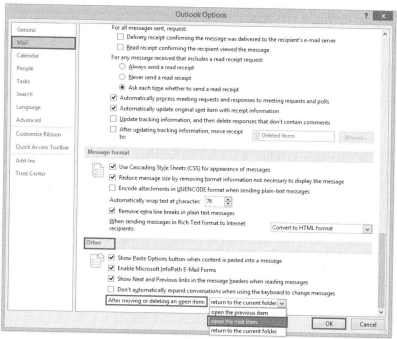

Figure 73

Step 5 – Click **OK**

Now when you delete a message, it will open the next message in the folder instead of returning to your Inbox. You will soon start to see some efficiency gains in your email management.

If you want to keep the message and go to the next message without going to Inbox just click the down arrow as shown or use the shortcut key **CTRL+>**

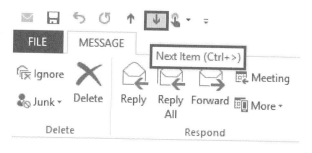

Figure 74

37.Out of Office

(Note: The out-of-office assistant only shows up if you are using a Microsoft Exchange® server. If you don't have an Exchange server, you can emulate the same process using Rules.)

For most users of Microsoft Outlook®, this feature is not new; however, it can be used as a productivity tool. For example, if you are involved in a project and do not want to be disturbed, you can set the Out of Office message as "Busy with critical projects, will respond to all e-mails tomorrow." This sets expectations and can be really effective.

One cool feature in Microsoft Office® 2010 and Microsoft Office 2013® is to set different Out of Office messages for internal and external customers. For example, you can list your cell phone for your team members when you head out on vacation, while pointing external customers to a team e-mail address or other appropriate direction.

If you have never set an Out of Office message, here are the steps for Microsoft Office® 2010:

Step 1 – Go to **File**, **Info**

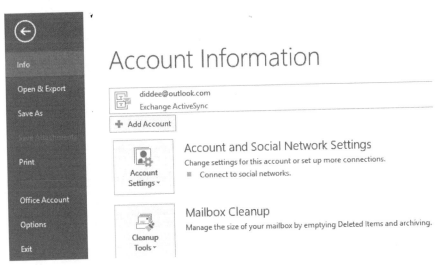

Figure 75

Step 2- Select **Automatic Replies** (Out of Office)

Automatic Replies (Out of Office)Use automatic replies to notify others that you are out of office, on vacation or not available to respond to e-mail messages.

Automatic Replies

Figure 76

You can set the following options:

- Select a specific time period

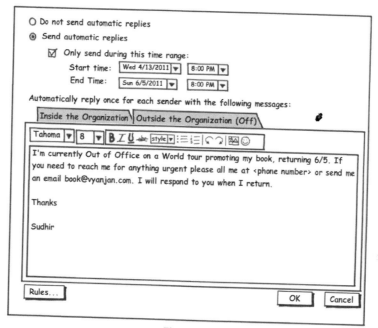

Figure 77

Use the "Inside" and "Outside the Organization" tabs to tailor your message.

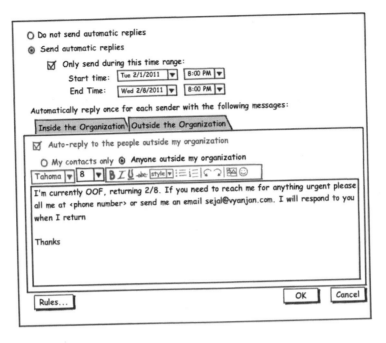

Figure 78

For people outside the company, you have the option of sending these responses to only your contacts, or to everyone.

Step 3 - Click OK

Step 4 - The Automatic Replies (Out of Office) will notify you that Automatic Replies are being sent.

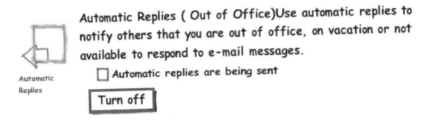

Figure 79

You can click Turn Off to stop sending automatic replies, or they will automatically cease if you entered an End Time when setting up the notification, which I suggest.

Figure 80

56

38.4 D's of E-mail handling

One of the best way to handle email is what is espoused by Sally McGhee, author of <u>Take Back Your Life!</u> Microsoft Press.

The 4 D's are

- Delete it
- Do it
- Delegate it
- Defer it

Delete it – Delete the email if it is informational only or does not relate to your objectives

Do it – If it takes less than 2 minutes

Delegate it – If someone else has to act on it, but add it to your follow up system

Defer it –Transfer it to a 1:1 category or calendar time to work on it, e.g. Custom Report Development or Detailed Product Launch Plan

Some Advanced Tips

This section has some advanced tips which are a collection of Outlook® tips and some best practices I have developed over the years, such as the Cool-Down Folder, Vacation Folder or things I have learned from highly efficient people like my manager who taught me what Extreme Presence means.

39.Quick Actions

- **New Item, New Email, and New Note -** Let's begin with a simple task: creating a new e-mail message in Microsoft Outlook®. If you are like a typical user, you create anywhere between 10 to 25 new e-mails a day, in addition to responding to others.

  To quickly create a new e-mail message just click **CTRL+N**.

- **Send a Message** - To send an e-mail message, click **CTRL + Enter**. Especially for those who send multiple e-mails in a day, the precious seconds saved from just these two tips will soon add up.

- **Create a New Office document** – This one is a killer tip hidden in plain view. For most people, spending 4 hours or more in Outlook® is not uncommon. So if you have to work on a new document or presentation, instead of scrolling to the ribbon at the bottom, just press **CTRL+SHIFT+H** and it presents the following screen for you to choose.

Figure 81

- **Launch the Font dialog box** – Often you are composing an email and you want to edit the font type, color etc. Instead of scrolling up to the ribbon all the time you can just type in **Ctrl+Shift+P** to launch the Font dialog box.

- **Launch the Style dialog box** – This is not used enough. If you type in **Ctrl+Shift+S** while typing an email in the body of the email it launches the Style dialog box.

40. Calendar Next day

"Let's meet two weeks from today, okay?" "John – Can you take the lead and schedule a meeting for all of us to meet next Friday?" Sounds familiar right? These are everyday conversations we have with our colleagues at work and then we go into the calendar to schedule the meetings.

Fortunately for us, our friends in the Outlook® team have thought about everyday life in far more detail than we could ever think of.

Here is how my Calendar appears on today's date

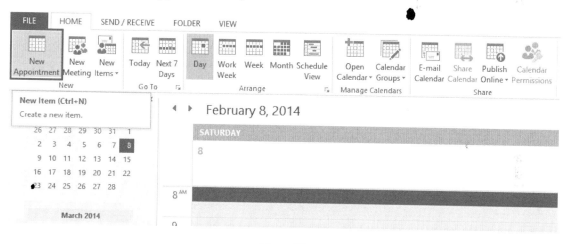

Figure 82

If I wanted to schedule a meeting for this Friday, in 9 days, or in three weeks, instead of trying to calculate the exact date by date picker I would just type in natural language in the date field and Outlook® will do the rest.

Hence for an appointment for this Friday just type "This Friday" in the Start Time and hit "Enter"

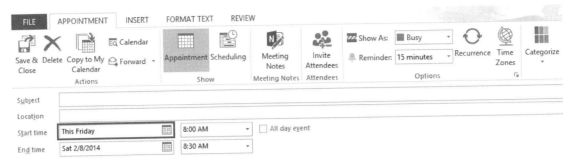

Figure 83

And the date automatically changes to 2/14/14

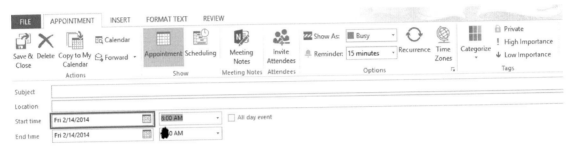

Figure 84

Try various combinations and you will be surprised. Try typing the following in the date fields:

- Christmas,
- Thanksgiving,
- in 4 weeks,
- in 18 days, etc.

and watch Outlook® do its magic. Once you get used to this, you will never go back.

41. Automatically Close the Message After Replying or Forwarding

If you are an office worker, you will invariably end up having 8 to 10 e-mails open, and after a while, you end up closing all of them. This can be really annoying and wastes a lot of time. One way to overcome this is to configure your Outlook® options to close your e-mail after you have replied or forwarded.

Step 1 - Launch **Microsoft Outlook®**.

Step 2 - Go to the top of the **Ribbon** and click **File**:

Step 3 - Click on the **Options** button:

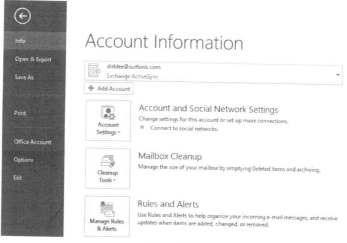

Figure 85

Step 4 - In the left pane, select **Mail**.

Step 5 - In the right pane, scroll down to the **Replies and forwards** section. Check the box - Close original message window when replying or forwarding

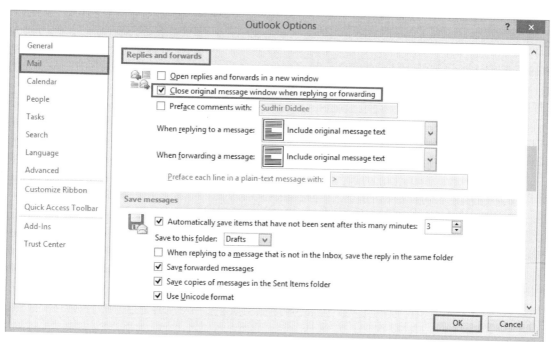

Figure 86

Step 6 - Click **OK**.

42.Insert Screenshot within an Outlook® message

Say you are working on a project or researching a product online. You might come across an image or information that you want to share with a friend or colleague. One way to share the image is to use the Snipping tool to e-mail the image (See Tip # 5). However, it might be just as efficient to insert the screenshot within Outlook®. Here is how it works.

Let us say you see the website shown below, and you get an idea that you want to run by your team.

Figure 87

To send it as a Screenshot within Outlook®, follow these steps:

Step 1 – Click on **File, Insert, Screenshot**

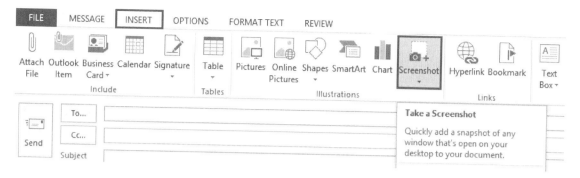

Figure 88

Step 2 – You will see all Active windows. Mouse over to select the window you want and **Left click.**

Figure 89

Step 3 – The whole screenshot is inserted in the body of the email.

Figure 90

Step 4 – This is optional: you can work with the formatting tool to crop the image, and only keep the section you want in the body of the email. The formatting tool bar is shown below:

Figure 91

And here is an example of an edited section of the screenshot:

Figure 92

Only one screenshot at a time can be added. To add multiple screenshots, repeat steps 1 and 2.

43.E-mail Delay

I have talked to many people and one of the universal reasons for stress is an email from the boss. It doesn't matter what the topic is; unless it is marked 'low importance,' people are tempted to read it no matter the hour and the heart rate goes up. And the higher you go up the ladder, the greater the impact of your email on the stress level of your organization.

Now, the other side of this issue is that the higher you go the harder and longer you work. Almost all the senior leaders I have had the opportunity to observe are not only highly accomplished and competent, but they supplement it with extremely hard work. Hence almost all of them are working weekends for a good portion of the year.

So how can a manager send important emails, without causing staff member's heartburn over the weekend? The answer is **Delay Delivery.** You can have the option of writing the e-mail but you can use the delay delivery option to set a time when the email is to be delivered. This way if you are sending non time-sensitive email, you can set the email to be delivered outside of the weekend/holiday dates. Personally I find it very useful to get things out of my to-do list but not to overwhelm my teams on weekend.

Here is how to do set delay delivery on an email.

Step 1 – Compose a message as usual. Click on **Options, Delay Delivery**

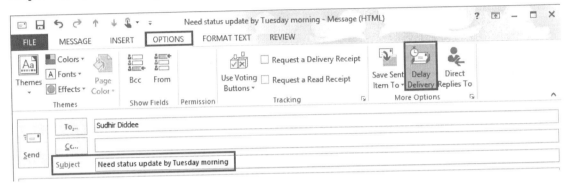

Figure 93

Step 2 – Set the Do Not Deliver Before option. Choose other conditions you need for the message.

Step 3 – Click **Close**

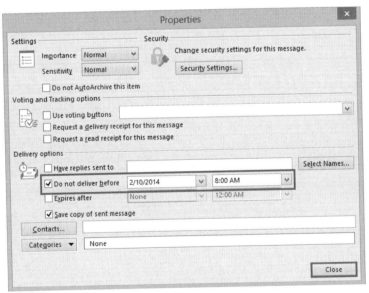

Figure 94

One caveat is that the e-mail is in your Outbox and will not be sent until the time set on the message. So you would need to send it from a PC that is connected all the time and will be online at the time you want the e-mail sent. If the PC goes to sleep, or you shut down and do not log in for a few hours until after the defined time, the email will be delayed further. One workaround is to ensure the PC is connected, have a screen saver in the background, and changing the settings to ensure the PC does not go to sleep. Then check your Outbox to ensure it has, indeed, been sent. With a bit of trial and error to adapt it to your own work style, you can really use this feature to improve the happiness of your team.

44. Creating a calendar entry from an e-mail

One of the top reasons most people who are overwhelmed by e-mail cannot manage time or e-mail is the urge to immediately act on every piece of email whenever they are checking e-mail. While in some cases it might be an email from your manager asking you about while s/he is in a meeting or has a time-sensitive request themselves. But more often than not, if you get a request like "Can you please review the attached slide deck and provide feedback?", you might be better off blocking some time on your calendar over the next couple of days to work on it and respond in a timely manner. This does two things:

- It is off your mind in the moment
- You commit to doing the work during a dedicated window of time in the near future and give it your undivided attention (no panic, and also no IM, Web, Phone, Facebook, Twitter, texting ☺)

Here is how to move an email to the calendar in the future

Step 1 – In the Inbox **Right click** while the pointer is on the email, and drag it down to the task bar on the Calendar tab of Outlook®

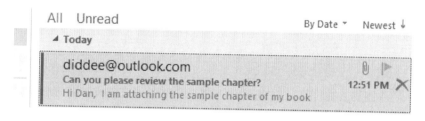

Figure 95

Step 2 – When you see a cross hair, release the Right Click and you are presented with 5 options. I like the option highlighted below where I am able to Copy the e-mail in the appointment as an attachment. This way when I sit down to work on the e-mail action item at the appointed time, I have all the information in the appointment.

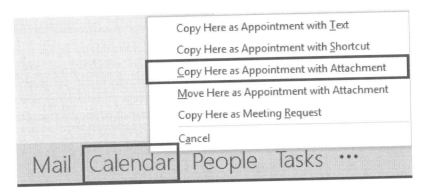

Figure 96

45.E-mail Filters

For many people in large organizations, a significant portion of the e-mail volume is generated from within the organization. However, you also end up using your work e-mail for signing up at conferences and other marketing-related information from time to time. They can all clutter your inbox and create **noise** in the inbox.

One way to filter the noise is to use FILTERS. If you use e-mail filters, you filter all e-mails coming from outside your company domain name in order to quickly clear up, review and delete those outside e-mails.

Here is how to set the filter for if I wanted to set a filter for all emails coming outside the @Microsoft.com domain.

Step 1 – Go to **View**, **View Settings**

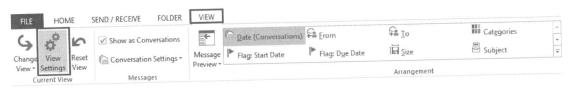

Figure 97

Step 2 – Click on **Filter**

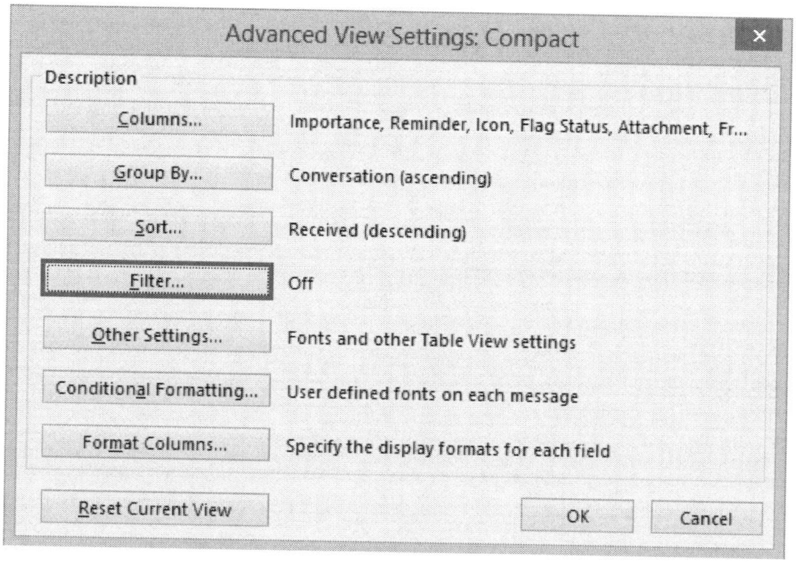

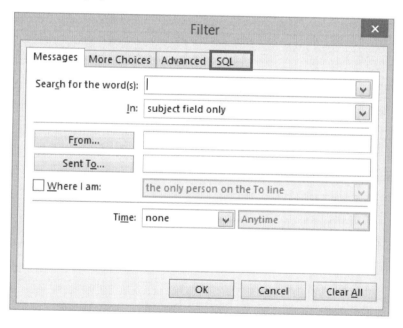

Figure 98

Step 3- Click on **SQL** to bring up the text box

Figure 99

Step 4 – In the text box enter the words below as it is- which essentially tells Outlook® to filter all emails that do **NOT** belong to the MS-Exchange organization

NOT ("http://schemas.microsoft.com/mapi/proptag/0x007D001E" ci_phrasematch 'X-MS-Exchange-Organization-AuthAs: Internal')

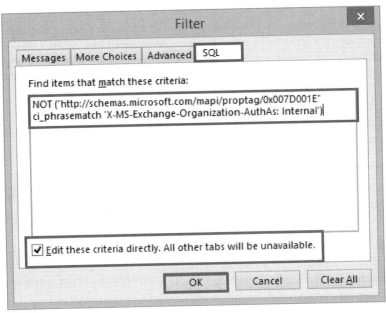

Figure 100

Step 5 Click to **OK** to save and name the view as "External" to reflect it shows all emails outside the domain

46.E-mail Group

Let us say you email a group of friends regularly. The scenario could be a weekend cycling club or alumni club or a few classmates you routinely email about your common interests. Instead of typing their addresses one by one, you can create a **Contact Group:**

Step 1- Click on the **People** Tab at the bottom and Click **New Contact Group**

Figure 101

Step 2 – Give the Contact Group a name; e.g.: Weekend Cartoonists or Cycling Century Trainers

Step 3 - You will be presented an option to Add Members. There are three options:

- From Outlook® Contacts
- From Address Book
- New E–mail Contact: A dialog box opens to manually add an e mail.

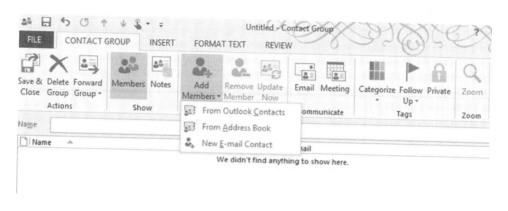

Figure 102

Step 4 - When all Members have been added, click **OK**

Now you can use this new group whenever you send a group e-mail.

47.Vacation E-mail

Here is a controversial but very effective e-mail management technique for people returning from any vacation longer than one week (though it can apply to that too). Every year I try to take a vacation of two to three weeks to India. It usually starts a week or so before Christmas and ends at the New Year. It helps that the e-mail volume is usually low at that time of year, but still I end up with about 2 weeks' worth of e-mail. I deliberately stop checking emails on vacation since it takes two to three days for work to get out of your head. At an average of 100 emails a day (give or take), it is perhaps 1200 - 1300 emails to take care of when I get back from vacation. There is no point in taking a vacation if you spend 2 days reading through e-mail.

Here is a technique which some of the people I have shared it with have found it useful as well:

- Before leaving for vacation move all e-mail to a **Pre-vacation** folder
- After coming back move all the email to a During **vacation** e-mail folder
- Next, sort the vacation e-mail by high importance– which are probably 5-10 e-mails at max and take care of them if they have not been acted upon already
- Read/reply to all e-mails sent by your management chain, after applying the Clean Up and reading it in Conversation view, to ensure you are responding knowledgeably to the latest thread

- Review all emails sent just to me, to get back to the senders
- For everything else, take care of it when you have extra time

Believe me, it is a very humbling experience to get the realization that you are not as indispensable as you think, and there is life beyond email. Also try to put yourself in the shoes of the sender. If you sent an email to someone and that person was on vacation for two or more weeks, you would either find someone else or put a note in your calendar to follow up when that person came back from vacation.

48. Cool Down folder

Every now and then you receive an email to which you are tempted to reply, later regretting it and possibly damaging the relationship or your own reputation.

One of the best ways to work around this is to have a folder called "Cool Down". Whenever there is an email that really gets the adrenalin rushing and you want to reply with a "stinker," hold off and move the email (and perhaps your hasty reply?) to the Cool Down folder.

Ideally you will get at most two to three such emails a year. So this folder is a kind of "fuse" to let you blow the steam. If you get more than your fair share of such emails – time to either change the way you work with others... or change the place you work.

49. Leadership Principles of E-mail Management

Another best practice is to have Team and Organization Service Level Agreements or SLA's. One of the best leadership principles I have seen practiced is by my manager. She has also set an example I have never seen any other executive do, which is to set an expectation for a 3-day rule. Unless the email is marked High importance or has a deadline called out in the email, the rule on the team is to reply within 3 days, and this is bi-directional. Anyone on the team can reply to her in 3 days as well.

This sets a different level of expectation on email management which allows folks not to be obsessed by email all the time and instead, focus on the business.

50. Extreme Presence

One of the intangible benefits of working at Microsoft is the immense amount of human talent that is concentrated in one place. You get to work with highly accomplished people day in and day out, each of whom are unique in their own way. I happen to work for one such individual, Gavriella Schuster. She is not only high energy and extremely productive, but the one thing that separates her from the rest is **EXTREME PRESENCE**. I observed her over a period of time and the way she manages her attention is to zone in on the meeting or interaction and capture its true essence into actionable insights.

51. Walk around and meet people

This tip comes from one of my mentors, Ryan. Ryan is one of the finest managers and people leaders, and not only is he highly effective, he is extremely light on email. In fact, I have modeled my email management largely on the lines of his email management system.

One of the best ways to manage email is to immerse yourself in the organization and people at work and off work. One in-person meeting will easily replace 25 e-mails. Not only will you have a much more productive work life, you will truly have a practical network, vs. the network on LinkedIn or Facebook.

Cheat Sheets

Microsoft Outlook® 2013

There several short cut keys for Outlook® for E-mail, Calendar, People or Contacts. Below I am listing some of my favorites which practiced for a couple of weeks will become second nature and will soon start to help you improve your productivity.

Task	Quick Key
New e-mail message	Ctrl+N
Find a message or other item	Ctrl+E
Expand or collapse the ribbon	Ctrl+F1
Create a meeting request	Ctrl+Shift+Q
Create a task	Ctrl+Shift+K
Create a note	Ctrl+Shift+N
Create a new Office document	Ctrl+Shift+H
Create an appointment	Ctrl+Shift+A
Advanced Find	Ctrl+Shift+F
Check names (in email)	Ctrl+K
Increase font size	Ctrl+Shift+>
Decrease font size	Ctrl+Shift+<
Open a received message	Ctrl+O
Open the Address Book	Ctrl+shift+B
Mark as Read/unread	Ctrl+Q/Ctrl+U
Open the MailTip in the selected message	Ctrl+Shift+W
Go to a date	Ctrl+G
Switch case (with selected text)	Shift+F3
Add bullets	Ctrl+Shift+L
Insert a hyperlink	Ctrl+K
Apply styles	Ctrl+Shift+S
Display font dialog box	Ctrl+Shift+P
Check spelling	F7
© www.vyanjan.com	

The Four Ds For Decision Making

Delete it

If it does not relate to your objectives

If you can find it somewhere else

If you will not refer to it in 3-6 months and it's not legal or HR

Do it (less than two minutes)

Respond and/or file

Delegate it

Send delegation and if needed, track in Waiting For or 1:1 Category

Defer it

Transfer to a 1:1, Deferred Actions Category or Calendar

For more information on how to improve productivity and work/life balance, contact us at info@mcgheepro.com or visit www.mcgheepro.com. Copyright ©2012 McGhee Productivity Solutions. All rights reserved.

Appendix

The Windows® Graphical User Interface

The diagram below shows the elements and standard terminology of the Windows® Graphical User Interface.

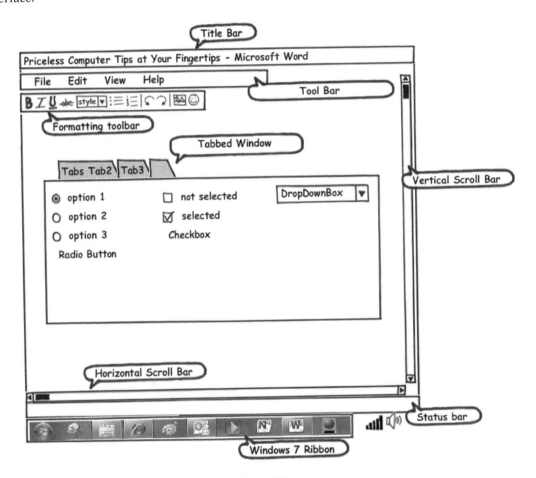

Figure 103

Note: If you are using Windows® 8 and Windows® 8.1 version the **Windows logo key** ⊞+**D** will take you to the familiar desktop

The Outlook® Graphical User Interface

The diagram below shows the elements and standard terminology of the Excel Graphical User Interface.

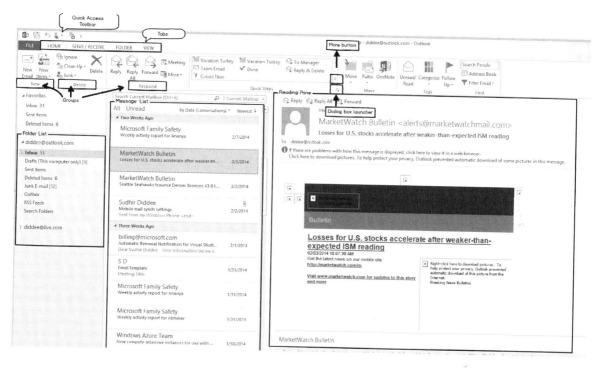

Figure 104

What is a Right Click on a mouse?

Most Windows® applications use the mouse's Right Click to activate very helpful, commonly used sub-menus or commands. The diagram below indicates the Right Click on a mouse.

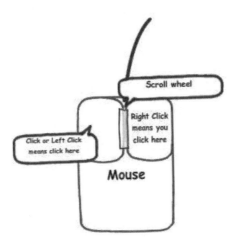

Figure 105

References

1. Kleiner Perkins Caufield & Byers's annual Internet Trends report
   http://www.kpcb.com/insights/2013-internet-trends

2. The 2013 edition of Tomi Ahonnen's Almanac[2] *2013 edition of the TomiAhonen Almanac*

3. Email Market, 2013-2017 , Editor: Sara Radicati, PhD; Principal Analyst: Justin Levenstein
   http://www.radicati.com/wp/wp-content/uploads/2013/09/Email_Market_2013-2017_Executive_Summary.pdf

4. The social economy: Unlocking value and productivity through social technologies, July 2012 | byMichael Chui, James Manyika, Jacques Bughin, Richard Dobbs, Charles Roxburgh, Hugo Sarrazin, Geoffrey Sands and Magdalena Westergren
   http://www.mckinsey.com/insights/high_tech_telecoms_internet/the_social_economy

5. Slow Down, Brave Multitasker, and Don't Read This in Traffic New York Times March 27th 2007 http://www.nytimes.com/2007/03/25/business/25multi.htm

6. JACKSON, T., DAWSON, R., WILSON, D., 2002. Case study: evaluating the effect of email interruptions within the workplace. IN: Conference on Empirical Assessment in Software Engineering, Keele University, EASE 2002, Keele, UK, April 2002, pp. 3-7.
   https://dspace.lboro.ac.uk/2134/489

7. Steve Ballmer*: MIX08 Conversation with* Guy Kawasaki http://www.microsoft.com/en-us/news/exec/steve/2008/03-06mix08.aspx

Useful Sites & Books

These links are provided for your convenience. The author has no responsibility for the content of the linked website(s) and books.

Microsoft Office® Site http://office.microsoft.com/en-us/
Lots of free templates, background designs and tips on using the various Microsoft Office Products

Microsoft Most Valuable Professional (MVP) Blog sites - http://www.mvps.org/links.html
A treasury of sites and links to possibly the most dedicated and selfless army of experts on various Microsoft products serving the community. Definitely it is my favorite site.

Extreme Productivity by Robert C. Pozen HarperCollins Publishers, 2011
http://bobpozen.com/

Take Back Your Life by Sally McGhee – I have learned a lot from Sally's book. It is definitely recommended, and is a must-have on any bookshelf. Learn more at www.mcgheepro.com

Outlook® Tips by Diane Poremsky, one of the most exhaustive tip sites on Outlook®:
http://www.outlook-tips.net/

How to Outlook® by Robert Sparnaaij an MVP for Office http://www.howto-outlook.com/

Book Ordering

If you would like to order more copies of this book, please send an email to diddee@outlook.com

Made in the USA
San Bernardino, CA
15 October 2014